Curious Questions and Answers about...

Super Scientists

Words by Robert Snedden

Illustrations by Fabrizio di Baldo

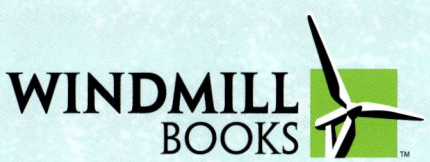

How do scientists work?

Every scientist uses a special way of asking and answering questions called the **scientific method**.

What is a vaccine?

Vaccines are medicines that can protect us against diseases. In 2020, **Professor Sarah Gilbert** and her team made the first successful vaccine against COVID-19.

Who Were the First Scientists?

Stargazing has its hazards!

Long ago, people learned how to do lots of clever things, like build pyramids, but they didn't know why things worked the way they did. To find the first scientists we have to go back thousands of years, to **ancient Greece**.

Eratosthenes measured the angles of shadows cast in two places on midsummer's day.

Who fell into a well?
Greek thinker **Thales** was interested in almost everything, including science, mathematics, and engineering. Once, he was concentrating so much on the stars that he fell into a well!

Who Grasped Gravity?

In the 1600s, **Isaac Newton** figured out that a force called gravity pulls things toward each other. So a tiny apple falls toward the big Earth.

Scientists do experiments to test their ideas.

Seeing an apple fall led me to the theory of gravity!

Newton worked out that gravity acts upon everything in the Universe.

Why doesn't the Moon fall from the sky?

The force of gravity holds the Moon in orbit around the Earth. The Moon travels fast enough to avoid crashing into the Earth but too slow to escape into space.

Moon's speed
Moon
Pull of Earth's gravity
Pull of the Moon's gravity
Earth

8

Which falls fastest?

In around 1590, Italian scientist **Galileo Galilei** dropped a heavy ball and a light ball from the top of a tower to see which would land first. People thought the heavy ball would fall faster, but both balls hit the ground at the same time.

So Galileo's experiment was right!

More than 400 years later, astronaut David Scott tried Galileo's experiment on the Moon! He proved that a feather falls as fast as a hammer when there is no air to keep the feather up.

Where can you find a space garden?

On the International Space Station. Scientists discovered that, because there is no gravity to tell them which way is up, plants in space use light to guide the way they grow.

The garden is called Veggie. Astronauts have been able to eat some of the plants grown!

9

Who Studies Energy and Matter?

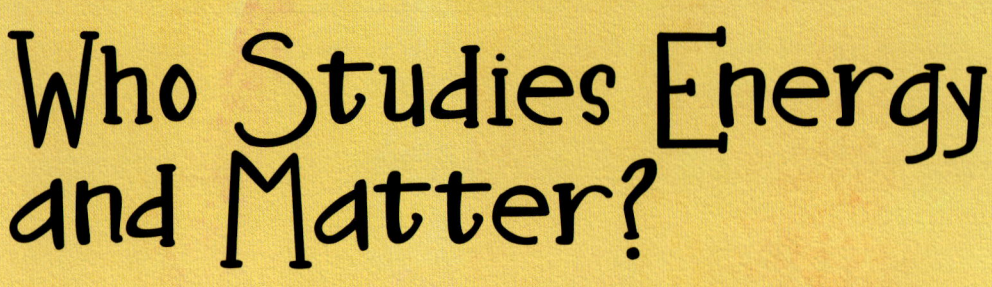

Scientists who study the matter that everything is made of and the energy that makes things happen are called physicists. Physics is one of the oldest of the sciences.

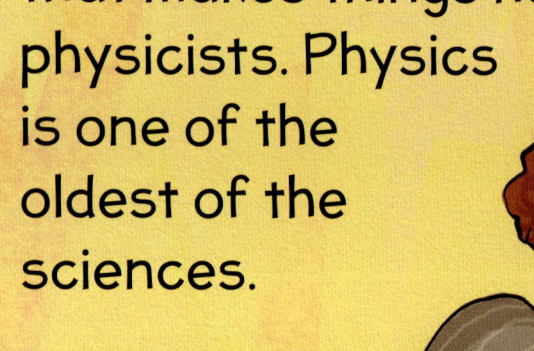

I discovered the radioactive elements radium and polonium.

Who investigated radioactivity?

Marie Curie was a famous scientist who studied a mysterious energy called radioactivity. Along with her husband Pierre, she discovered two new elements in 1898.

How did X-rays help?

Marie Curie also invented a mobile X-ray machine to help treat wounded soldiers in World War 1. It could be driven to the battlefield and allowed doctors to see inside the bodies of patients.

Marie and her daughter, Irene, trained women volunteers as X-ray operators.

Who saw the light?

Albert Einstein was a genius. He worked out that nothing can travel faster than light. He showed that time and space could change, depending on how fast you were going when you measured them! Einstein changed the way we think about the Universe.

This is my most famous equation!

$E=mc^2$

Who is looking into the atom?

As well as being famous for his television programs explaining science, **Professor Brian Cox** also carries out important research into what makes up atoms, the tiny building blocks of matter.

What Are Things Made Of?

Chemistry is all about substances, called chemicals, that everything, including us, is made of. Scientists who study what happens when different chemicals mix together are called chemists.

The shape shown in Photo 51 proved that DNA has a twisted ladder-like structure.

Photo 51 revealed what DNA actually looks like.

Who took Photo 51?

Rosalind Franklin's X-ray photographs in 1952 helped to discover the structure of DNA. DNA is like an information store in all living things that determines how they look and function.

How can we get things organized?

The basic substances that make up everything are called the chemical elements. In 1869, chemist **Dmitri Mendeleev** worked out a way of organizing them all in a big table that showed which ones had similar properties.

Periodic Table

The Periodic Table is still being updated as scientists discover more elements.

Super-tough Kevlar has about 200 uses!

What plastic is stronger than steel?

In 1965, American chemist **Stephanie Kwolek** invented Kevlar, a type of plastic that is five times stronger than steel. Kevlar is used in lightweight bicycles, aircraft, spacesuits, and bulletproof vests.

Did You Know?

As well as being a great physicist, **Galileo** also discovered the four largest moons of the planet Jupiter.

Callisto, Ganymede, Europa, and Io are known as the Galilean moons!

Galileo discovered the moons with a telescope he built himself.

Isaac Newton's three laws of motion describe how everything in the Universe moves, from tennis balls to stars.

The Sun is at the center of the Solar System, not us!

People used to think that the Sun went around the Earth until, in the 1500s, **Nicolaus Copernicus** explained that Earth and the other planets go around the Sun.

X-rays were discovered accidentally by German physicist **Wilhelm Roentgen** in 1895.

In the 1860s British doctor **Joseph Lister** showed that simple hygiene like washing your hands can help prevent diseases spreading.

French chemist **Louis Pasteur** proved that bacteria can be the cause of harmful diseases.

Ada Lovelace Day is held each year to celebrate women in STEM.

The very first computer program was written by **Ada Lovelace** more than 150 years ago!

The Nobel Prize is awarded for great scientific discoveries. **Marie Curie** is one of only five people to have won it twice!

I won for Physics in 1903 and Chemistry in 1911.

Who Is Finding Out About the Living World?

Chimps use sticks to "fish" for termites.

Scientists who study living things are called biologists. There are lots of different kinds of biologist. For instance, botanists study plants and zoologists study animals.

Jane Goodall

Termites

Conservationists like Jane work to protect animals and our habitats.

Do chimpanzees make tools?

Jane Goodall spent many years carefully watching chimpanzees to see how they behave. She was the first person to see that chimpanzees can make and use tools.

I also studied coprolites — fossilized poop!

In 1823, Mary discovered the first complete skeleton of a plesiosaur, a long-necked marine reptile.

Who Looks Back in Time?

Planet Earth, and the plants and animals that live on it, have not always been the same. Geologists study the way the Earth changes and palaeontologists find out about life long ago.

Who found a strange monster?

Mary Anning was one of the first people to study life from long ago. When she was just 12, Mary found the body of an ichthyosaur, an extinct reptile that lived in the sea over 190 million years ago. Her brother found the skull!

What is the theory of evolution?

Charles Darwin had the idea that living things change, or evolve, over many years to make them better suited to their surroundings. The ones that were best suited were most likely to survive.

We all evolved from the same species of bird!

These birds have different beaks because they evolved to eat different foods.

Darwin collected 14 species of bird from the Galápagos Islands in 1835.

Did dinosaurs care for their young?

In the 1970s, palaeontologist **Jack Horner** found a nest of 15 baby dinosaur fossils. The nest showed that the adults of these dinosaurs, called Maiasaura, looked after their young.

A fossil of a baby Maiasaura coming out of its egg.

Who Is Looking Out in Space?

Scientists who study the planets, stars, and other objects in space are called astronomers. Space scientists design spacecraft to explore far beyond the Earth.

Comet

Pulsar

At first, it was thought that the pulsars' signals could be coming from alien "little green men"!

Can you spot a comet? **Caroline Herschel** was a talented astronomer. She discovered objects in space that no one had seen before, including eight comets.

I helped to build the huge radio telescope that picked up signals of pulsars!

There is a huge black hole at the center of the Milky Way!

Caroline Herschel

Jocelyn Bell Burnell

Stephen Hawking

If a comet flies near the Sun, gas and dust stream away from its core, forming shining tails.

Black hole

What happens inside a black hole?

Nobody really knows! A black hole has such an immense pull of gravity that nothing can escape it, not even light. **Professor Stephen Hawking** was one of the world's greatest experts on these mysterious objects.

Who discovered pulsars?

Pulsars are unusual stars that spin very quickly and give out pulses of high-energy radiation. They were discovered by **Jocelyn Bell Burnell** in 1967, when she was just 24 years old.

Andromeda galaxy

Hubble Space Telescope

How big is space?

Space is very big – and it is getting bigger! Astronomer **Edwin Hubble** discovered that the Universe is expanding like a huge balloon.

Edwin Hubble

The Hubble Space Telescope was named after me!

23

Who Knows How the Human Body Works?

Medical scientists have made amazing breakthroughs in understanding the human body, and why problems sometimes happen.

What's that smell?

Humans can pick out a trillion different scents. Scientists **Linda Buck** and **Richard Axel** discovered how the nose and the brain work together in the sense of smell.

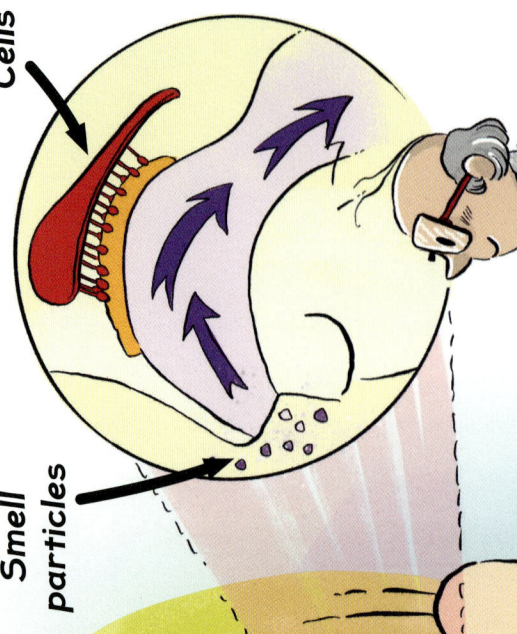

Cells

Smell particles

Smell particles are detected by tiny cells in your nose, which then send signals to your brain.

Everything you do, think, and say is controlled by your brain.

What's going on inside your head?

Neuroscientists study our brain and nervous system. **Padma Srivastava** pioneers treatments for serious conditions.

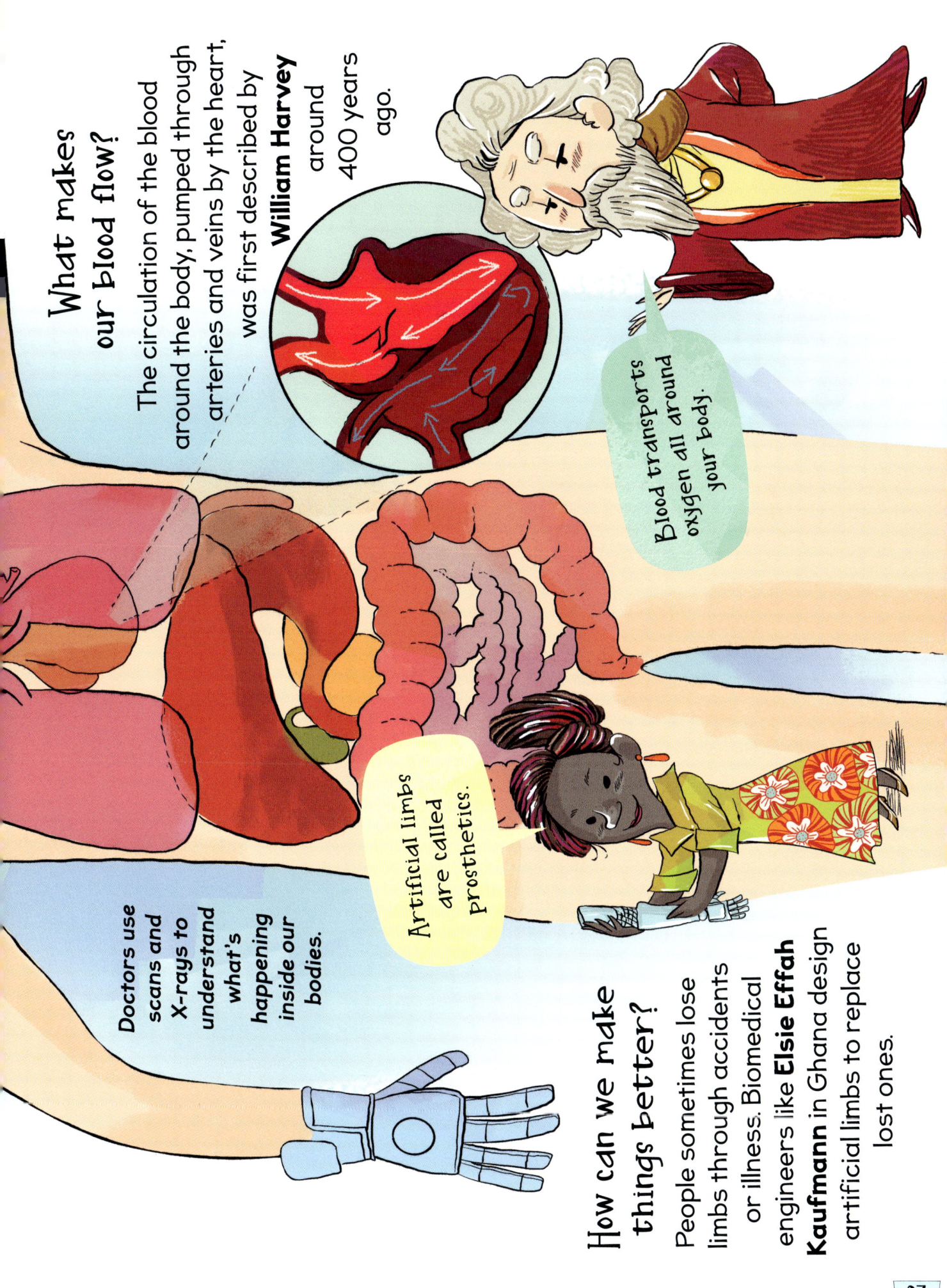

Can Scientists Save the Planet?

Climate change is something that concerns all of us. Environmental scientists can help us find ways of tackling the problem.

Through the work of scientists, we now know that climate change makes wildfires and storms more likely.

What's happening to the climate?

Climatologist **James Hansen** was one of the first scientists to show how changes in the atmosphere are causing the Earth's temperature to increase, changing the climate.

What can we do to help?

Environmentalists like **Wangari Maathai** in Africa led the way in the fight for the environment. She started the Green Belt Movement, aiming to plant millions of trees to replace those that have been lost.

You could be an environmentalist too!

What's happening in the ocean?

Changes aren't just happening in the air and on the land. Marine biologists like **Sylvia Earle** are showing what a terrible effect climate change is having on ocean life as well.

i'm a marine biologist. I study life in the ocean.

A Compendium of Questions

Is there life on other planets?
There probably is, but we haven't found it. Yet!

Can we travel in time?
Some scientists think that it might be possible, but it would be very, very difficult and beyond what we can do at the moment.

I might need a bigger cake!

Why do we sleep?
We spend about a third of our lives asleep, but scientists aren't sure why. Sleep gives the body time to rest, make repairs, and store memories.

Is it possible to live forever?
Scientists are looking into ways to slow down the process of ageing. So we might live longer, but perhaps not forever.

How many scientists are there?

"It's always useful to share ideas in science!"

"There are around 9 million scientists in the world. That's a lot of people looking for answers to tricky questions. Could you be one of them one day?"

Do we know more about the Moon or the ocean?

Nearly three quarters of the Earth is covered by ocean. At the moment we have better maps of the Moon than we have of the bottom of the ocean.

How many different living things are there?

Nobody knows for sure. So far scientists have named 1.2 million different species (kinds) of plants and animals, but there could be as many as 10 million that we haven't named yet.

"Some species may go extinct before they're even discovered."

Why do we yawn?

Surprisingly, scientists are still puzzling over that one. Perhaps it helps get more blood to the brain to make us more alert, but we're just not sure!

Published in 2026 by Windmill Books,
an Imprint of Rosen Publishing
2544 Clinton St.
Buffalo, NY 14224

First published in 2023 by Miles Kelly Publishing Ltd
Copyright © Miles Kelly Publishing Ltd 2023

Publishing Director   Belinda Gallagher
Creative Director   Jo Cowan
Editorial Director   Rosie Neave
Senior Editors   Sarah Carpenter, Amy Johnson
Designers   Joe Jones, Karen Doughty
Image Manager   Liberty Newton
Production   Elizabeth Collins
Reprographics   Stephan Davis

Cataloging-in-Publication Data
Names: Snedden, Robert, author. | di Blado, Fabrizio, illustrator.
Title: Super scientists / by Robert Snedden, illustrated by Fabrizio di Blado.
Description: Buffalo, NY : Windmill Books, 2026. | Series: Curious questions and answers about...
Identifiers: ISBN 9781538399040 (pbk.) | ISBN 9781538399057 (library bound) | ISBN 9781538399064 (ebook)
Subjects: LCSH: Scientists--Juvenile literature.
Classification: LCC Q147.S643 2026 | DDC 509.2--dc23

All rights reserved.

No part of this book may be reproduced in any form without permission
in writing from the publisher, except by a reviewer.

Printed in the United States of America

CPSIA Compliance Information: Batch #CSWM26
For Further Information contact Rosen Publishing at 1-800-237-9932

Find us on